Joan Jackson has loved writing since she was a small child, so very long ago. When she had her own two little boys, their love of her stories spurred her writing of children's stories into a passion. They would sit be her side asking for stories about such things as bunnies in jewel-lined caves. What a pleasure to create word pictures in their small minds.

When the world recently quieted and people stayed in their own homes for long stretches of time, Joan's story writing imagination took flight more than in recent years. She derives great pleasure in writing stories.

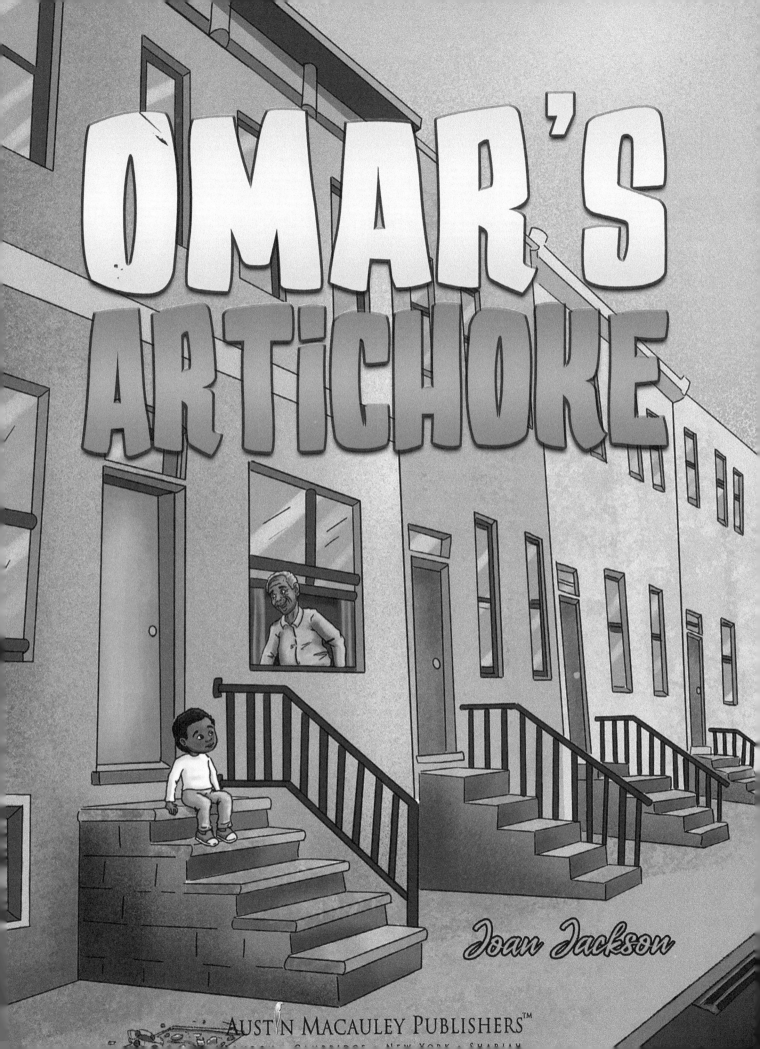

OMAR'S ARTICHOKE

Joan Jackson

AUSTIN MACAULEY PUBLISHERS™

Ordering Information
Quantity sales: Special discounts are available on quantity purchases by corporations, associations, and others. For details, contact the publisher at the address below.

Publisher's Cataloging-in-Publication data
Jackson, Joan
Omar's Artichoke

ISBN 9781685623630 (Paperback)
ISBN 9781685623647 (Hardback)
ISBN 9781685623654 (ePub e-book)

Library of Congress Control Number: 2023910442

www.austinmacauley.com/us

First Published 2023
Austin Macauley Publishers LLC
40 Wall Street, 33rd Floor, Suite 3302
New York, NY 10005
USA

mail-usa@austinmacauley.com
+1 (646) 5125767

My deepest gratitude is for my sweet husband Byron and our now-grown sons Robin and Alex, who were often the spark of stories of the past. And now I have a daughter at last with our Mel. My heart is with this family of mine.

And for the many dear friends I treasure around the world,
With thanks.

Thank you to Austin Macauley Publishers for making my lifelong dream come true

Omar lived in a big gray city. He lived with his grampa in a building on 47th Street where there weren't any trees or bushes.

There was a small square of dirt beside his steps, about 16 inches square, where he played with his tiny plastic cars and pretended to dig for dinosaur bones.

On a day in spring, his grampa handed him a rumpled brown paper bag. "Open it Omar, it's a special thing for you."

Omar eagerly opened the bag but inside,
there was just a little wilted green plant.
"What is it?"

"An artichoke plant. Let's put it right here, and we can watch it grow."

They scraped away some of the dry dirt, making a hole the size of the little silvery green plant's roots. Omar ran to bring some water in an empty milk jug. His grampa and he set the roots into the dirt, poured in some water, and covered the hole with more dirt.

Omar didn't know anything about artichokes. This was just a little plant to grow, a summer adventure for the five year old boy.

The next day, Omar's grampa brought his used coffee grounds outside and carefully sprinkled them around the little plant. Omar gave it some water.

Every day, Omar sat on his steps near his artichoke plant. People on the street asked him what he was growing. And each day, the artichoke plant grew a little bit more.

It grew taller than the first step. It grew taller than the second and third step. It grew wider than the small patch of dirt.

The mailman had to walk a slight detour around it as he walked by. And every morning, Omar and his grampa put coffee grounds and water on the dirt.

Before long, the dirt became soft and felt different. A neighbor called it "soil" and explained to Omar the difference.

Before long, the plant was taller than Omar. He stood on the steps to reach its top. He watched as the artichoke plant grew a big bud on top. The bud was green and round, and covered with spiky leaves.

Mr. Gino from the corner store came for a visit and told Omar this was a carciofi. "Car cho fee?" Omar asked.

"Yes, that means artichoke in Italian. When I was a little boy, we ate those every summer. When they're ready to eat, I'll show you how."

Omar thought about this, but couldn't imagine eating the spiky hard thing.

Little buds began to form on stalks where the leaves grew out of the main stalk. Omar had to stand on the top step to reach the top of the plant. Omar was so surprised when the biggest bud opened into a huge purple spiky flower that looked like a thistle!

Omar, his grampa and Mr. Gino picked the little artichoke buds, and Mr. Gino prepared them for dinner.

It was Omar's most delicious meal ever,
because he grew the artichokes all
by himself.

The End!

9 781685 623647